Key to the earthworms of the UK and Ireland

By Emma Sherlock

BRINGING
ENVIRONMENTAL
UNDERSTANDING TO ALL

© FSC and Natural History Museum, London 2012
ISBN 978 1 908819 02 4
Occasional Publication 150

 **NATURAL HISTORY MUSEUM**

The vision of the Natural History Museum, London is to advance our knowledge of the natural world, inspiring better care of our planet. The Angela Marmont Centre for UK Biodiversity at the Museum is for anyone with an interest in UK natural history.

To contact the Museum's Identification and Advisory Service, e-mail amc-enquiries@nhm.ac.uk, telephone 020 7942 5045, or join the online forums at www.nhm.ac.uk/natureplus.

Contents

Acknowledgement	iv	**Species accounts**	28
Introduction	1	*Allolobophora chlorotica*	28
Scope of the key	1	*Allolobophoridella eiseni*	29
Ecology	5	*Aporrectodea caliginosa*	29
Anatomy	7	*Apporectodea cupulifera*	30
Sampling techniques	8	*Aporrectodea icterica*	30
Recording data and labelling	9	*Aporrectodea limicola*	31
Preservation techniques	11	*Aporrectodea longa*	31
Microscope work	14	*Aporrectodea rosea*	32
How to use the key	14	*Dendrobaena attemsi*	33
Main features explained	15	*Dendrobaena hortensis*	33
Tanylobic or epilobic head	15	*Dendrobaena octaedra*	34
Male pore	16	*Dendrobaena pygmaea*	34
Clitellum/saddle	16	*Dendrobaena veneta*	35
Tubercula pubertatis (TP)	17	*Dendrodrilus rubidus*	35
Setae/chaetae	17	*Eisenia fetida*	36
Counting segments	18	*Eiseniella tetraedra*	36
Key to the earthworms of the UK and Ireland	19	*Helodrilus oculatus*	37
		Lumbricus castaneus	37
Quick earthworm comparison chart	26	*Lumbricus festivus*	38
		Lumbricus friendi	38
		Lumbricus rubellus	39
		Lumbricus terrestris	39
		Microscolex phosphoreus	40
		Murchieona muldali	40
		Octolasion cyaneum	41
		Octolasion lacteum	41
		Satchellius mammalis	42
		Sparganophilus tamesis	42
		References	43

ACKNOWLEDGEMENTS

I would like to thank the Earthworm Society of Britain's committee members for helping with the testing of this key as well as anyone who has been on one of our many training courses.

Thank you to The Natural History Museum for their support, especially the Soil Biodiversity Group: Paul Eggleton, Daniel Carpenter, David Jones and Kelly Inward; and to the Zoology Department especially Miranda Lowe, Clare Valentine and Andrew Cabrinovic. A very big thank you to Louise Berridge for artistic support, including drawing Figs 1, 2 and 4, and Phil Hurst and Harry Taylor for photography.

Thanks to Stewart Lee and Sally Mcphee for producing the datasheet used by the author and themselves on fieldwork in Nicaragua (Fig. 7). Also thanks to Reginald Sims, my predecessor at the Natural History Museum and a huge inspiration. Without the key he developed with B.M. Gerard, I would never have broken into the world of British earthworms.

Csaba Csuzdi, Chris Lowe, Kevin Butt, Aidan Keith, Gordon Paterson, Daniel Carpenter, Paul Eggleton and Miranda Lowe reveiwed the text after it had been tested and made important suggestions for improvements.

Finally, thanks to Csaba Csuzdi and Victor Pop for answering my endless questions.

This key was partially financed by the Nature Conservancy Council as part of its Commissioned Research Programme.

INTRODUCTION

Earthworms are some of the most commonly recognised soil invertebrates. They are found in urban parks, gardens, woodlands, farmland and even these days, with the introduction of worm bins, in our own homes. I think that most people appreciate the role that earthworms play in decomposition and healthy soils, but not many take the time to stop and study these highly important animals.

Surprisingly perhaps, the UK has a long history of earthworm scientists. Most are not household names, despite their great works, although one who is widely known is Charles Darwin. One of the most celebrated scientists to be born in the UK, he devoted years of his life to the study of earthworms and his last, and in his lifetime, biggest selling book, published in 1881 was entirely devoted to them.

Despite all of this, earthworms are still some of the least recorded animals on the planet. In the UK and Ireland we have only 27 species and are in the fortunate position that all can be distinguished by external features alone, making their identification possible for everyone. We have very little clue about their distribution and exact habitat preferences (Carpenter *et al*, 2011). To get a full picture of what is happening around the UK in wet and dry soils, heaths, mires, and rotting logs we need to have many more recorders in many more places.

My main aim in producing this key is to encourage more people to record the earthworms around the UK and Ireland. While there have been good identification keys for British species in the past (and up until 2002 they accounted for all the Irish earthworms as well) I have realised when taking courses that people still struggle to get to grips with the main features. I hope this key, which is illustrated with photographs at every stage, will help.

I also wanted to put together for the first time in one key all the earthworms that are likely to be found naturally in the soils in the UK and Ireland regardless of family, and update the taxonomy which has changed since the last keys were produced.

SCOPE OF THE KEY

This key is for the identification to species level of mature preserved specimens of all species of earthworms in the UK and Ireland. The species listed are those that might be found living freely in the soils around the UK (Table 1 in Sherlock & Carpenter, 2009, with corrected omissions). The worms that are only found in hot greenhouses around the country, but have so far been unable to colonise the soils outside of these environments, are included in the list but excluded from the key. Taxonomic names are updated from Csuzdi & Zicsi (2003) and Blakemore (2008).

It is, unfortunately, not possible to identify accurately the majority of species live. A field key to the live specimens of the commoner species was produced as part of the Open Air Laboratories (OPAL) project in 2009, which is useful for narrowing down choices, but for accurate identification preserving the worms is necessary. The worms also need to be mature so all structures can be seen. In all cases it is recommended that you check your identification with the comprehensive species pages at the back of this book (pages 28-42). Occasionally damaged or abnormal worms, which are harder or impossible to identify, will be found. Irish species are covered, which include *Aporrectodea cupulifera*, recorded in Ireland for the first time in 2002.

Table 1. Complete list of earthworm species recorded in the UK and Ireland.
Part 1 lists the species found living in natural environments. Part 2 lists the species recorded from artificial habitats. Updated list from: Sherlock, E. & Carpenter, D. (2009).

Part 1: earthworm species living in natural environments				
Family	Genus	Species	Authority	Notes
Lumbricidae	*Allolobophora*	chlorotica	(Savigny, 1826)	There are two colour morphs of this species, pink and green
Lumbricidae	*Allolobophoridella*	eiseni	(Levinsen, 1884)	Called *Lumbricus eiseni* by Sims & Gerard 1999 but *Allolobophoridella* by Blakemore 2005 and Csuzdi & Zicsi 2003
Lumbricidae	*Aporrectodea*	caliginosa	(Savigny, 1826)	
Lumbricidae	*Aporrectodea*	cupulifera	(Tetry, 1937)	Found in Ireland 2002
Lumbricidae	*Aporrectodea*	icterica	(Savigny, 1826)	
Lumbricidae	*Aporrectodea*	limicola	(Michaelsen, 1890)	
Lumbricidae	*Aporrectodea*	longa	(Ude, 1885)	
Lumbricidae	*Aporrectodea*	rosea	(Savigny, 1826)	
Lumbricidae	*Dendrobaena*	attemsi	(Michaelsen, 1902)	
Lumbricidae	*Dendrobaena*	hortensis	(Michaelsen, 1890)	Called *Eisenia hortensis* by Sims & Gerard 1999 but *Dendrobaena* by Blakemore 2005 and Csuzdi & Zicsi 2003
Lumbricidae	*Dendrobaena*	octaedra	(Savigny, 1826)	
Lumbricidae	*Dendrobaena*	pygmaea	(Savigny, 1826)	
Lumbricidae	*Dendrobaena*	veneta	(Rosa. 1886)	Called *Eisenia veneta* by Sims & Gerard 1999 but *Dendrobaena* by Blakemore 2005 and Csuzdi & Zicsi 2003
Lumbricidae	*Dendrodrilus*	rubidus	(Savigny, 1826)	
Lumbricidae	*Eisenia*	fetida	(Savigny, 1826)	
Lumbricidae	*Eiseniella*	tetraedra	(Savigny, 1826)	

Continued

Family	Genus	Species	Authority	Notes
Lumbricidae	*Helodrilus*	*oculatus*	Hoffmeister, 1845	
Lumbricidae	*Lumbricus*	*castaneus*	(Savigny, 1826)	
Lumbricidae	*Lumbricus*	*festivus*	(Savigny, 1826)	
Lumbricidae	*Lumbricus*	*friendi*	Cognetti, 1904	
Lumbricidae	*Lumbricus*	*rubellus*	Hoffmeister, 1845	
Lumbricidae	*Lumbricus*	*terrestris*	Linnaeus, 1758	
Acanthodrilidae	*Microscolex*	*phosphoreus*	(Duges, 1837)	
Lumbricidae	*Murchieona*	*muldali*	(Omodeo, 1956)	Named *miniscula* by Sims & Gerard 1999, but later that year *muldali* (an earlier synonym of *miniscula*) was resurrected as a separate species; *miniscula* is a southern species, *muldali* a northern one
Lumbricidae	*Octolasion*	*cyaneum*	(Savigny, 1826)	
Lumbricidae	*Octolasion*	*lacteum*	(Örley, 1881)	Called *tyrtaeum* by Sims & Gerard 1999 but this was based on what is widely regarded as a false synonymy made by Gates
Lumbricidae	*Satchellius*	*mammalis*	(Savigny, 1826)	
Sparganophilidae	*Sparganophilus*	*tamesis*	Benham, 1892	

Part 2: earthworm species recorded from artificial envionments

Family	Genus	Species	Authority	Where found
Eudrilidae	*Eudriloides*	*durbanensis*	Beddard, 1893	Kew Gardens, from Durban
Eudrilidae	*Eudrilus*	*eugeniae*	(Kinberg, 1867)	Kew Gardens. Beddard 1906
Eudrilidae	*Helodrilus*	*lagosensis*	Beddard, 1891	Kew Gardens, from Lagos. Beddard 1891
Eudrilidae	*Hyperiodrilus*	*africanus*	Beddard, 1891	Kew Gardens, from Africa. Beddard 1891
Glossoscolecidae	*Diachaeta*	*bardadensis* (in Sims & Gerard as *Trichochaeta bardadensis*)	(Beddard, 1892)	Kew Gardens, from Barbados

Continued

Family	Genus	Species	Authority	Where found
Glossoscolecidae	*Hesperoscolex*	*hesperidium*	Beddard, 1894	Kew Gardens from cases of soil from Trinidad and Jamaica. Beddard 1891
Glossoscolecidae	*Pontoscolex*	*corethrurus*	(F. Muller, 1857)	Kew Gardens. Beddard 1906
Megascolicidae	*Amynthas*	*alexandri*	Beddard, 1901	Kew Gardens, soil from Calcutta. Type
Megascolicidae	*Amynthas*	*corticis*	(Kinberg, 1867)	North Wales and Kew. Beddard 1890
Megascolicidae	*Amynthas*	*gracilis*	(Kinberg, 1867)	Kew Gardens, soil from Barbados and Mauritius
Megascolicidae	*Amynthas*	*morrisi*	(Beddard, 1892a)	Kew Gardens, soil from Mauritius
Megascolicidae	*Amynthas*	*rodericensis*	(Grube, 1879)	Kew Gardens, soil from China. Beddard 1892
Megascolicidae	*Anisochaeta*	*celmisiae*	(Jamieson, 1973)	Scotland
Megascolicidae	*Anisochaeta*	*minor*	(Spencer, 1900)	Scotland
Megascolicidae	*Metaphire*	*californica*	(Kinberg, 1869)	Kew Gardens, a case of soil from Barbados and Hong Kong
Megascolicidae	*Metaphire*	*posthuma*	(Vaillant, 1868)	Kew Gardens
Megascolicidae	*Metaphire*	*schmardae*	(Horst, 1883)	
Megascolicidae	*Perionyx*	*excavatus*	Perrier, 1872	Hertfordshire and Chelsea Gardens
Megascolicidae	*Polypheretime*	*taprobane*		Kew Gardens
Moniligastridae	*Drawida*	*barwelli*	(Beddard, 1886)	Kew Gardens
Ocnerodrilidae	*Eukerria*	*rubra*	(Friend, 1918)	Botanical Gardens Oxford by Friend 1916
Ocnerodrilidae	*Gordiodrilus*	*ditheca*	Beddard, 1892	Kew Gardens
Ocnerodrilidae	*Gordiodrilus*	*dominicensis*	Beddard, 1892	Kew Gardens
Ocnerodrilidae	*Gordiodrilus*	*elegans*	Beddard, 1892	Kew Gardens, soil from Lagos
Ocnerodrilidae	*Gordiodrilus*	*robustus robustus*	Beddard, 1892	Kew Gardens
Ocnerodrilidae	*Ilyogenia*	*africana*	Beddard, 1893	Kew Gardens, soil from Durban

Continued

Family	Genus	Species	Authority	Where found
Ocnerodrilidae	Nematogenia	lacuum	(Beddard, 1893)	Kew Gardens, soil from Lagos
Ocnerodrilidae	Ocnerodrilus	occidentalis	Eisen, 1878	
Octocheatidae	Dichogaster	affinis	(Michaelsen, 1890)	Kew Gardens, soil from Lagos
Octocheatidae	Dichogaster	bolaui	(Michaelsen, 1891)	Swimming pool in Ireland 2006
Octocheatidae	Dichogaster	saliens	(Beddard, 1893)	Kew Gardens
Octocheatidae	Eutyphoeus	nicholsoni	(Beddard, 1901)	Kew Gardens, Beddard 1901
Octocheatidae	Trigaster	minima	Friend, 1911	Kew Gardens, soil imported from possibly Carribean. Friend 1911

ECOLOGY

The importance of earthworms to soil health and structure has long been recognised; Aristotle described them as the 'intestines of the earth' due to the way they break down dead organic matter, which releases nutrients back into the soil. Earthworms till and aerate the soil, allowing plant roots to move more freely and oxygen to penetrate. They are often referred to as ecosystem engineers. Although much could be said about earthworms and their ecology, this section will be kept brief as this is primarily a guide to sampling, preservation and identification. However, some basic earthworm ecology is useful to understand the different sampling techniques that need to be undertaken.

Researchers often split earthworms into three or four ecological groups, although research continues into how rigidly they conform to these groupings. However, these groups are still a useful way to understand the different roles these animals have. As this guide concentrates on 27 species, Blakemore's 2008 model or the Lee's 1959 model have not been used; instead what follows is based on Bouché's model (1971, 1977). In addition, the purely composting worms have been grouped separately.

Group 1: the composters

This group can sometimes overlap a little with group 2: the epigeic worms. They are mainly found in compost heaps or in areas of very high organic matter such as under cow pats in a field. Usually no soil is consumed.

They are red in colour and often have a stripy appearance when stretched out.

UK and Ireland species: *Eisenia fetida, Dendrobaena veneta, Dendrobaena hortensis*.

Group 2: the epigeics

These are usually surface dwelling earthworms found under leaf litter, in rotting logs, and in epiphytes in trees. They feed directly on the decaying matter. Little or no soil is consumed.

They again are usually red in colour (in the tropics they can even be blue).

UK and Ireland species: *Dendrobaena attemsi, Dendrobaena octaedra, Dendrobaena pygmaea, Dendrodrilus rubidus, Lumbricus castaneus, Lumbricus festivus, Lumbricus rubellus, Satchellius mammalis.*

Group 3: the endogeics

These are the soil dwellers with horizontal burrows. These worms rarely come to the surface and consume the soil itself.

They are usually much less pigmented and are more grey/pink or even greenish in colour.

UK and Ireland species: *Allolobophora chlorotica,* most *Aporrectodea caliginosa, Aporrectodea cupulifera, Aporrectodea icterica, Aporrectodea limicola, Aporrectodea rosea, Eiseniella tetraedra, Helodrilus oculatus, Murchieona muldali, Octolasion cyaneum, Octolasion lacteum.*

Group 4: the anecics

These are the deep burrowing worms that use the vertical burrows. They often come up to the surface at night and draw leaves and other dead plant material down into their burrows. Some soil can be ingested.

They are often a deep red or even black colour dorsally and are always large worms.

UK and Ireland species: the nocturna morph of *Aporrectodea caliginosa, Aporrectodea longa, Lumbricus friendi, Lumbricus terrestris.*

Further reading on earthworm ecology

Blakemore, R.J. (2008). Seeking consensus on main categories of ecological strategies of earthworms. Advances in Earthworm Taxonomy III. *Proceedings of the 3rd International Oligochaeta Taxonomy meeting.* pp 129-136.

Edwards, C.A. (2004). *Earthworm ecology.* CRC Press (2nd edition).

Edwards, C.A. & Bohlen, P.J. (1996). *Biology and ecology of earthworms.* Chapman and Hall (3rd edition).

Lee, K.E. (1985). *Earthworms: their ecology and relationships with soils and land use.* Academic Press Sydney. p 411.

ANATOMY

Earthworms are in the phylum Annelida, class Clitellata and subclass Oligochaeta. Therefore they are segmented worms which possess a clitellum (or saddle). To understand how earthworms function, some of their internal anatomy, which is readily seen on dissection, is included here.

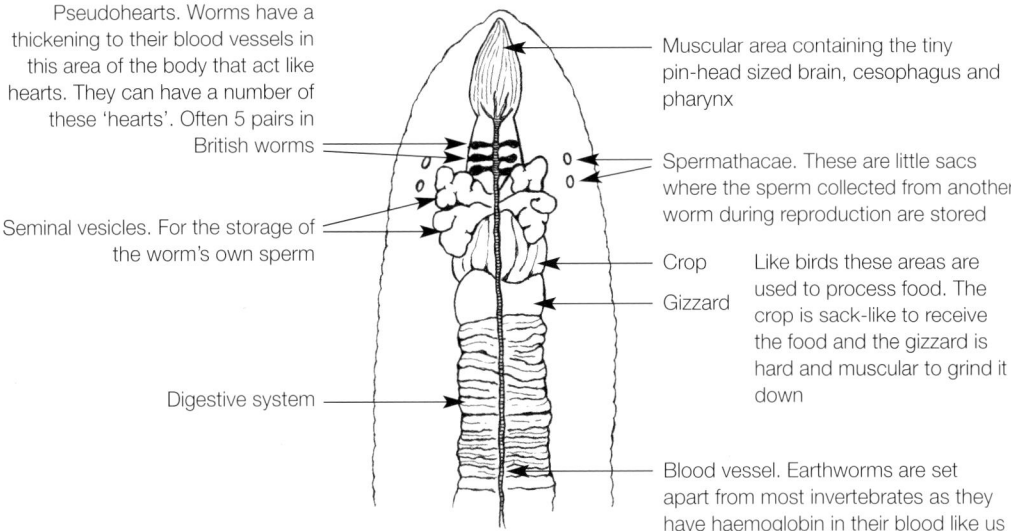

Figure 1. Internal features of an adult earthworm

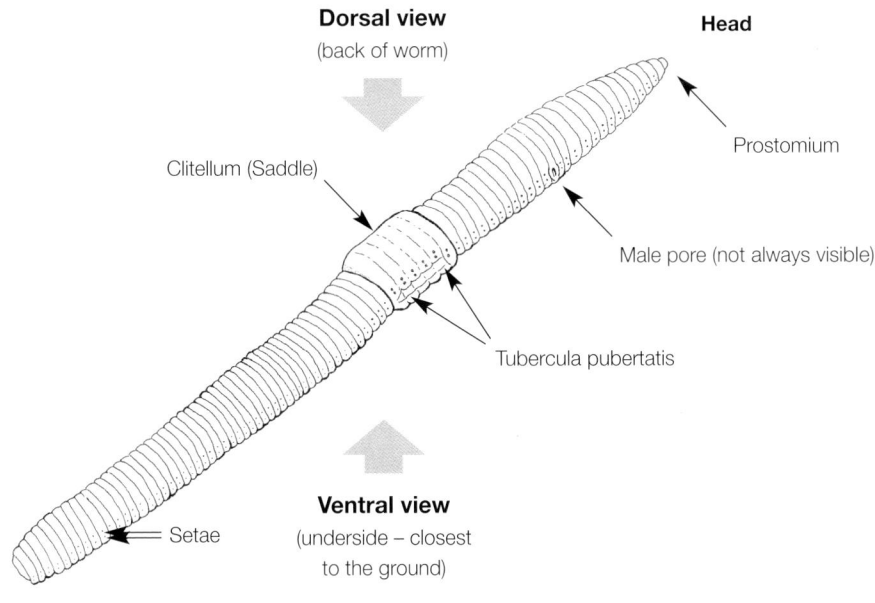

Figure 2. External features of an adult earthworm

SAMPLING TECHNIQUES

A number of different sampling methods are required to get a comprehensive picture of all the different species of earthworm to be found in a particular habitat.

The soil

When digging for earthworms the best method is to dig out blocks of soil. First mark a 25 x 25 cm square with a spade (in practice about a spade and a half by a spade and a half). Consistency in sampling is essential so that different sites can be compared at different dates; particularly important if any ecological studies are to be undertaken.

Once the square has been marked, as quickly as possible dig the block out, preferably whole. Depending on the soil and density of roots and stones this may not always be possible. Aim for a depth of at least 10-15 cm.

Figure 3 (right). Mark a 25 x 25 cm square with a spade

Figure 4 (below). Dig out a block of soil and place it on a plastic sheet

Place the block on a tray or plastic sheet (such as a bin liner) and then start hand sorting. A good hand sorting technique is to break pieces off the block of soil and then very finely sort through your fingers. Some earthworm adults are only a centimetre or two long, and when in diapause (a type of hibernation for earthworms when conditions are too dry) the worms can be curled up into tight knots. They can also be located in the roots of the grass.

Figure 5 (right). Hand sorting: break pieces of soil off from the block and finely sort through using fingers

Microhabitats

Not all worms are found in the soil. So it is also important to search the surrounding environment for other earthworm niches. Look under leaf litter, stones, and any objects lying on the ground. Also target rotting logs, looking underneath and inside, especially under the bark.

Vermifuge

The best way to gather the anecic worms is to pour an irritant on the ground. A vermifuge is particularly good for places where you cannot dig, such as golf courses. Formalin is the most effective solution used, but as it is a hazardous chemical we do not recommend it. As long as the soil is not too waterlogged or extremely dry, then a solution of mustard powder dissolved in water is the best alternative. For a 25 x 25 cm square, 4 large heaped tablespoons in 2 litres of water is recommended. It can take up to ten minutes for the last of the worms to emerge. Be aware that they do not always emerge in the square you poured the mustard solution into. Check that worms have emerged fully before picking them up. Do not pour the solution over too large an area as it needs percolate right down into the soil.

RECORDING DATA AND LABELLING

When in the field collecting worms, always record and label as you go along. You will never remember the localities the worms were found in when you get home. The more information you have about a specimen, the more valuable it is.

Always take with you in the field:

- Sampling tubes for collecting earthworms
- Paper labels to be placed with the worm inside the tube (preferably special paper that is alcohol resistant and conservation grade such as Resistall; poor quality papers can break up)
- Pencil (special Rotring pens with alcohol resistant ink are better; pencil can fade over time, but in the field pencil is fine)

Figure 6. Sampling for earthworms in Vietnam.

Figure 7. An example datasheet used by the author while sampling for earthworms in Nicaragua.

- Scissors
- GPS (or a compass and local map)
- Notebook (there are special waterproof notepads which are very useful) or data recording sheets which prompt you to fill in all details

As soon as you get to your first site, write in the notebook or on your data sheet as much information as you can. Location must be recorded as precisely as possible (ideally longitudes and latitudes from GPS) but map grid references are fine. Habitat information is also important, so record for example whether you are in a woodland or grassland, and what plants you can see nearby. Record the date.

Use a separate sampling tube for each individual microhabitat sampled (e.g. from a log, the soil, leaf litter, etc.), with its own label put in the tube.

PRESERVATION TECHNIQUES

If the worms have been brought to the lab live and needed for a long-term reference collection, go straight to the 'in the lab' instructions on page 13. Otherwise please follow one of the 'in the field' methods below.

In the field

Method 1: the quick way

For UK and Irish species, long-term storage for dissection is not required for identification, so you can use this method if the worms are not needed for a reference collection. This method is also useful if you are collecting worms primarily to gather molecular data (DNA work).

You will need:
- Good quality tubes which won't crack
- Alcohol 80-100%

The quickest way to preserve worm samples is to place them straight into 80-100% alcohol as soon as they are collected. Do not fill the tube more than a quarter full with worms. Worms have a large quantity of fluid in them, so when they die they release those fluids into the tube and dilute the alcohol. Change the alcohol in the tube after 5 minutes and then again after 15 minutes. If worms are needed for DNA studies they should be placed in 100% alcohol (N.B. most absolute alcohol is actually about 96% rather than 100%, but this is fine). If not needed for molecular studies, it is best to use 80% alcohol to prevent the worms from becoming too brittle.

This method will keep your worms safe. However, they may end up bent in an awkward position which can make identification a bit more difficult later. They will also lose all colour, and they will not be as firm and easy to handle as those preserved in the method below.

Method 2: best practice

You will need:
- Good quality tubes which won't crack
- Alcohol 80-100%
- Tupperware tub (leak proof)
- Water
- Formalin 4% (optional). Formalin is a proven carcinogen. Safety procedures need to be followed when using this substance. See note * on page 13

Step 1: **Relaxation and anaesthetising.** Place the worms straight into a tub of 30% alcohol. This can be made up beforehand and carried with your kit as long as it is leak proof. This will help 'clean the worms' as well as relaxing and anaesthetising them. Leave them in this for approximately 5 minutes – but no longer as the worms must not die in this completely relaxed state. When the worms become more sluggish take them out.

Step 2: **Straightening and fixing.** Worms can be straightened while they are fixing. Suitable fixatives are:

1) 80-100% alcohol if formalin is either unavailable or undesirable for the user (and if DNA work might be required then the worms should be in 96-100% alcohol at all times)

2) 4% formalin is the best fixative but not good for preserving DNA

Although the best straightening tool is a 'Pop' worm tray (see Figure 8 and page 13 for instructions on how to make this) it is generally not practical for use in the field unless it is made very light. Instead worms can be straightened to a certain degree using any rulers, rocks or twigs that are available. While they are still 'floppy' from the anaesthetising, lie

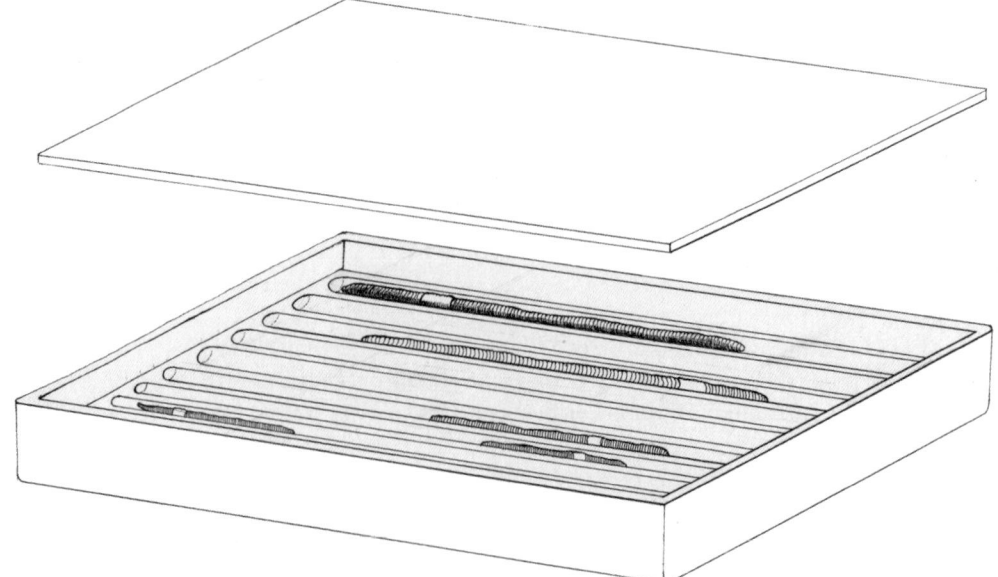

Figure 8. A 'Pop' worm tray in use.

them between two straight objects (or lay them straight in the upturned lid of your Tuppaware box, along the edge of the rim), then add the fixative of high percentage alcohol or formalin. Let the fixative pool a little around the worm. Ideally worms should be kept this way for a long period of time but since this is not possible in the field, place your worm in your collecting tube after 5-10 minutes. This should make the worms easier to work with than the quick method outlined above.

In the lab

Follow these procedures if the worms have been brought to the lab live. They include instructions on long-term preservation for a reference collection.

You will need:
- Good quality tubes which will not crack
- Alcohol 80-100%
- Alcohol 30%
- 4% formalin (optional). Formalin is a proven carcinogen. Safety procedures needed to be followed when using this substance. See note * below
- Worm tray (optional)

Step 1: **Relaxation and anaesthetising.** Place the worms straight into a tub of 30% alcohol. This will help 'clean the worms' as well as relaxing and anaesthetising them. Leave them in this for approximately 5 minutes – but no longer as the worms must not die in this completely relaxed state. When the worms become more sluggish take them out.

Step 2: **Straightening and fixing.** Worms can be straightened while they are fixing. The best fixatives are:

1) 80-100% alcohol (if formalin is either unavailable or undesirable for the user) and if DNA work might be required. In which case the worms should be in 96-100% alcohol at all times)

2) 4% formalin, if colour needs to be preserved but the worm will not be needed for molecular work

The best straightening tool is a 'Pop' worm tray (designed by the Pop family in Romania). This is a block of wood or plastic with furrows chiselled into it (see Figure 8), which you can make yourself by using a soldering iron on plastic or a file on wood. Worms can be fixed within the furrows of the tray by pouring the fixative over the tray and covering with a lid to prevent the worms from drying out.

Leave the worms in the fixative for as long as is possible, ideally at least 2 days. Then transfer to the preservative. A 4% formalin solution is the best, but an 80% alcohol solution is fine for long-term storage if preferred. If it is possible to have a few months to a year in 4% formalin first, this will help the colour of the worm to be preserved in the longer term and keep the worm firm.

---

* Formalin: When using formalin or formaldehyde a number of safety procedures need to be followed. Read the hazard information on the bottle. Only work in a well ventilated area (otherwise specialist breathing masks are required), use rubber or plastic gloves and wear safety glasses.

Long-term storage

For long-term storage worms should be placed in either:

1) 80% alcohol

2) 4% formalin

As outlined on page 12.

The best long-term storage jars are made of glass and have ground glass stoppers. Suitable glass jars can be sourced from Dixon Glass (www.dixonglass.co.uk). Grease the seal with vaseline or soft white paraffin.

Figure 9. Long-term storage of an earthworm specimen.

Microscope work

A low powered microscope or stereomicroscope is needed for identifying earthworms. Make sure the microscope is set up correctly before starting.

Place the preserved worm in a plastic or glass clear Petri dish and always **completely immerse** the worm in water or alcohol. When water is being used, leave the water in a bottle overnight if possible so any bubbles have settled.

When looking at a particular character, especially setae, which can be difficult to locate, manipulate the specimen and light sources to find the best angle for viewing. Features which cannot be seen at first can become quite apparent after changing the angle of view or direction of the light.

Forceps and seekers are the best tools for manipulating or turning the worm (see Figure 10).

How to use the key

Only adult worms can be accurately identified to species using this key. To distinguish an adult worm from a juvenile look for a clitellum (or saddle). If no clitellum (or any markings in this area) is present then all that can be determined is whether the worm has a tanylobic or epilobic head. Worms with a tanylobic head are in the genus Lumbricidae.

If the saddle is not fully developed but some markings are visible that could be a TP (see explanation on page 17) then this juvenile earthworm could still potentially be identifiable.

You will need to be familiar with where on an earthworm's body the features highlighted below are to be found. Refer to the general biology section (pages 15-18) where the external anatomy is highlighted if you are unsure.

Main features explained

Tanylobic or epilobic head

First locate the head end: the head is the end that is closest to the male pore and clitellum (saddle).

The head must be viewed dorsally (looking down from the top, not from the underside).

Often this will involve manipulating the worm to get it in a suitable position. Do not be scared to hold the head down with forceps to get a good view.

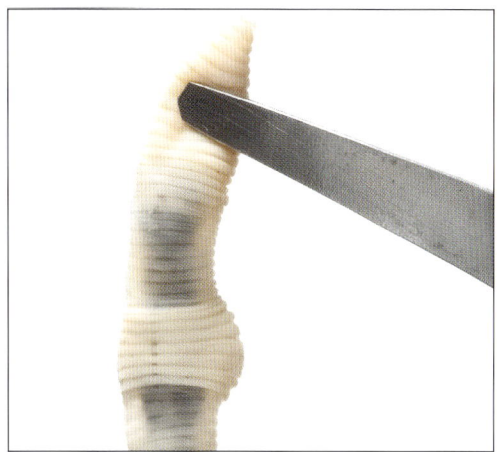

Figure 10.

Figure 11. Tanylobic head.

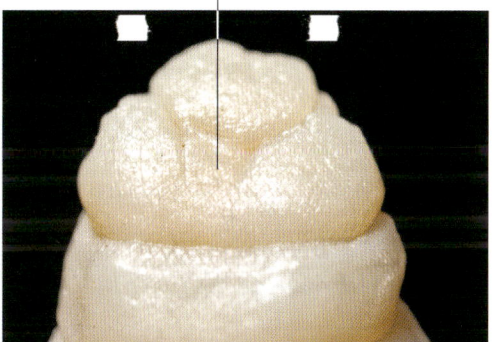

Figure 12. Epilobic head.

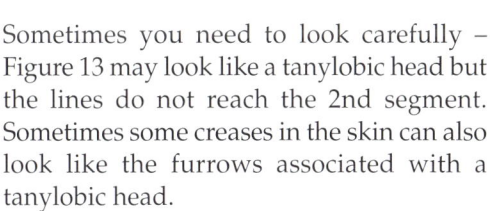

Sometimes you need to look carefully – Figure 13 may look like a tanylobic head but the lines do not reach the 2nd segment. Sometimes some creases in the skin can also look like the furrows associated with a tanylobic head.

If unsure key out in both sides of the key and check species accounts pages carefully.

Figure 13.

Male pore

In the Lumbricidae family this pore is found on segment 13 or 15 (Figure 14). It can be very large encompassing the surrounding segements.

Or it can even look a bit more like a slit than a pair of small lips (Figure 15).

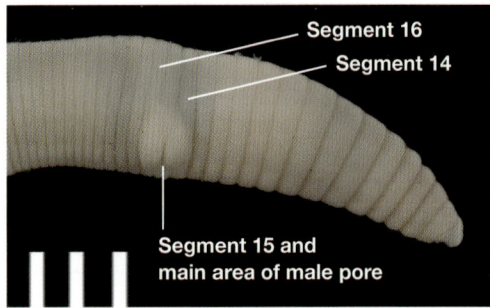

Figure 14. *Allolobophora chlorotica*.

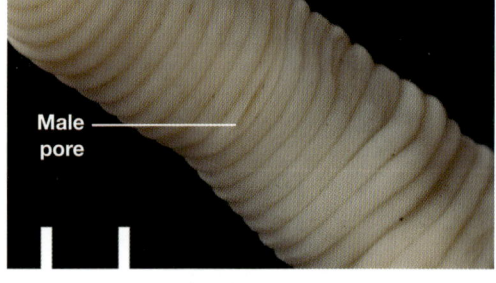

Figure 15. *Eiseniella tetraedra*.

Clitellum/saddle

The clitellum or saddle of an earthworm is important in reproduction. It produces the mucus used in cocoon formation.

The presence or absence of a clitellum indicates whether it is a juvenile or adult worm. The positioning of the saddle is very important when identifying worms (Figures 16 and 17).

Figure 16. Juvenile worm. No clitellum present.

Figure 17. Adult worm. Clitellum present.

Tubercula pubertatis (TP)

These are the markings, lumps, lines, swellings or 'sucker like discs' that are to be found on the lateral undersides of the clitellum.

Figure 18.

Figure 19. *Aporrectodea longa*.

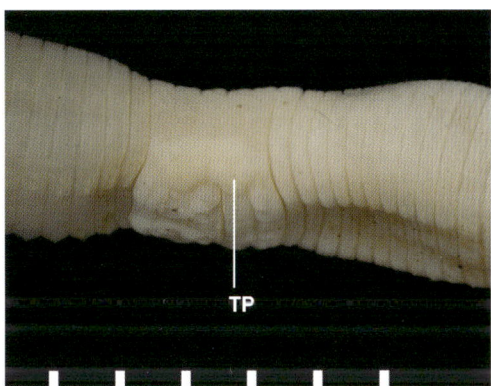

Figure 20. *Aporrectodea caliginosa*.

Setae/chaetae

Earthworms all have small setae on each segment. In the Lumbricidae family there are 4 pairs per segment and whether these are widely or closely paired after the clitellum is sometimes used diagnostically. This can be the hardest character to see. Adjusting the microscope lighting and looking closer to the tail end of the worm can help.

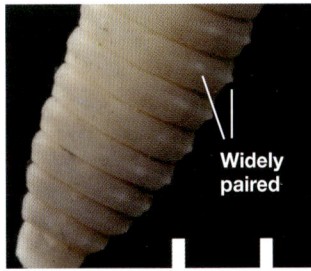

Figure 21. *Dendrobaena octaedra*.

Figure 22. *Dendrobaena veneta*.

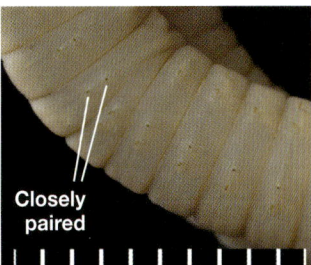

Figure 23. *Lumbricus terrestris*.

Counting segments

This is something you will often have to do. To get started, the first segment to count is the first full ring. Do not count the prostomium.

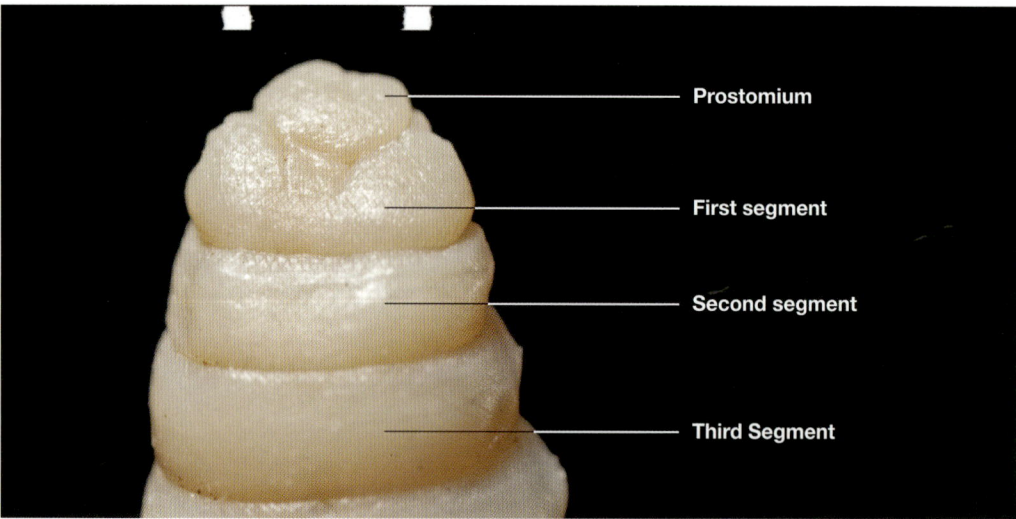

Figure 24. Counting the first few segments from the head.

If you have already counted the 13 or 15 segments to the male pore, you do not need to count from the head again when counting segments to the clitellum and TP, just keep counting from that point.

Some segments can have confusing furrows through them. If unsure, look for the setae ridges to count segments.

Be careful when counting segments on the clitellum – the segments often become wider.

Figure 25. Segments can become wider on the clitellum.

KEY TO THE EARTHWORMS OF THE UK AND IRELAND

If identifying earthworms for the first time please consult the section 'How to use this key' (p. 14) before getting started.

1. Is the head tanylobic or epilobic?

Please view worm dorsally for this character – see page 15.

- Tanylobic .... Go to question 2

  Head-line of prostomium meets the 2nd segment.

Check: When colour is visible, worms with tanylobic heads are red. If in life your worm was not red in colour you have gone wrong – check the head again.

- Epilobic ...... Go to question 5

  Head-line of prostomium does not meet the 2nd segment but stops short.

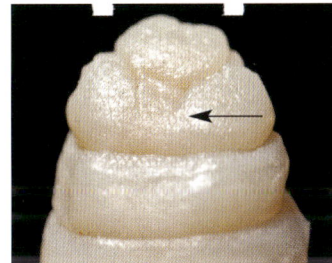

2. Does the clitellum (saddle) start on segment 29 or before?

Best to view worm dorsally for this character.

- Yes .... Go to question 3

- No .... Go to question 4

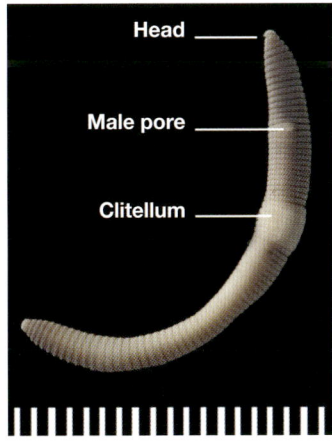

Read all 4 options

3. Does the TP fall on segments:

TP can be seen on lateral side of clitellum, best to view worm ventrally.

- 27 or 28 to 31 .... *Lumbricus rubellus* (p. 39)

- 29 to 32 .... *Lumbricus castaneus* (p. 37)

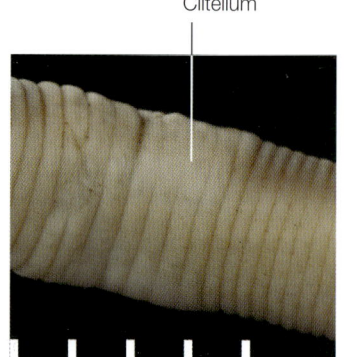

Check: Double check in case the TP on the worm is there but just hard to see. This worm should be approximately 4-6 cm long with a clitellum spanning segments 29 to 32 or 33.

- TP not visible (clitellum on segments 24 or 25 to 32 or 33) .... *Allolobophoridella eiseni* (p. 29)

- None of the above .... Go back to question 1
  Recheck the head and recount segments.

Read all 3 options

4. Does the TP fall on segments:

- 32 or 33 to 36 or 37 .... *Lumbricus terrestris* (p. 39)

- 34 to 36 .... *Lumbricus friendi* (p. 38)

- 35 to 38 .... *Lumbricus festivus* (p. 38)

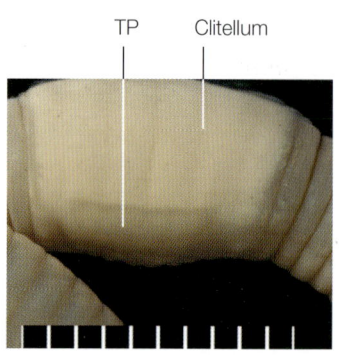

Lumbricus terrestris

5. Does the clitellum (saddle) start on segment 13?

- Yes .... *Microscolex phosphoreus* (p. 40)
- No .... Go to question 6

Check: If the clitellum starts on 15 you may have *Sparganophilus tamesis*. This is a very rare worm in the UK and might not now be present here. Check species account on page 42 for more information.

6. Is the male pore on segment 13?

- Yes .... *Eiseniella tetraedra* (p. 36)
- No .... Go to question 7

Male pore

Check: The male pore can sometimes be small and look like an extra furrow in the segment.

7. Does the clitellum (saddle) start on segment 30 or before?

- Clitellum starting on segment 30 or before .... Go to question 8

- Clitellum starting on segment 31 or after .... Go to question 22

Read all 3 options

8. Is there a TP?

- TP present and starting on segment 31 .... Go to question 9

- TP present but not starting on segment 31 .... Go to question 10

- No TP present .... *Murchiona muldali* (p. 40)

See check box

Check 1: *M. muldali* is a very small grey/pink worm. The clitellum is on segments 27-33. It is usually just 1.5-4 cm long. If your worm does not match this description then the TP may just be hard to see. Please check the worm again.

Check 2: There is a rare form of *Dendrodrilus rubidus*, in which the TP is absent or very hard to see, which would key out here. It is a red worm with its clitellum on segments 25-27 to 31-32, and setae widely spaced. See page 35 for more information on this species.

Read all 3 options

9. Is the TP:

- 3 'sucker like' discs or 3 distinct lumps on 31, 33 and 35 .... *Allolobophora chlorotica* (p. 28)

    In life a green or pink worm – 'stumpy' in appearance.

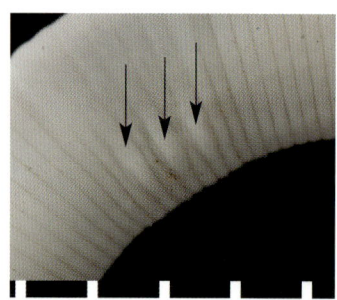

- A thin band on segments 31 to 33 (can sometimes be an indistinct raised area) .... *Dendrobaena octaedra* (p. 34)

    In life a small red worm.

- 2 'humps' over the area of segments 31 to 33 .... *Apporectodea caliginosa* (p. 29)

    In life a grey/pinky worm, generally quite large. One rare morph can be very large and dark in colour.

Check: If your worm has a TP just starting on 31 but the main area of the TP is 32-34 and it is a large worm with a dark head you are likely to have *Aporrectodea longa*. Please go to question 12.

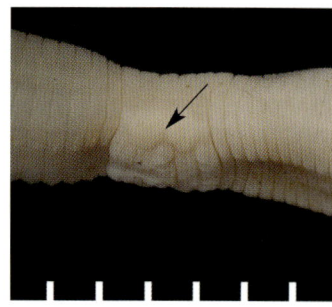

10. Are the setae closely paired?

- Closely paired .... Go to question 11

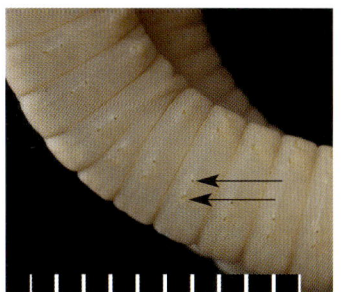

- Widely paired .... Go to question 17

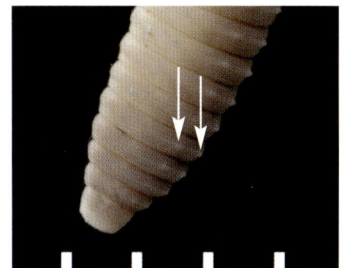

Tip: When looking at setae its best to look near the tail end of the worm, they often stand out better here. **Always** look after the saddle, never at the head end.

11. Does the TP start on or after segment 30?

- TP on or after 30 .... Go to question 12

- TP before 30 .... Go to question 13

12. Does the TP fall on segments:

- 31 or 32 to 34 .... *Aporrectodea longa* (p. 31)

- 33 to 34 .... *Aporrectodea limicola* (p. 31)

13. Does the TP start on segment 27 or 28?

- Yes .... Go to question 14

- No .... Go to question 15

Check: check carefully here that the TP starts on these segments and **not** 29.

14. Does the TP have 2 humps or suckers on segments 28 and 30?

- Yes .... *Aporrectodea cupulifera* (p. 30)

Check: so far only recorded in Ireland **not** in Britain.

- No .... *Eisenia fetida* (p. 36)

Check: these are composting worms rarely found outside of the compost bin or areas rich in organic matter.

15. Does the clitellum start on:

- Segments 21, 22 or 23 .... Go to question 16
- Segments 25 or 26 .... *Apporectodea rosea* (p. 32)

Check 1: if the TP is not visible and the clitellum falls on segments 26/27-33/34, you most probably have *Murchieona muldali* (p. 40).

Check 2: *Aporrectodea rosea* has a TP on segments 29-31 (occasionally just 29-30).

16. Does the TP start before segment 25?

- Yes .... *Eiseniella tetreadra* (p. 36)
  (a rarer form with the male pore on 15 not 13)

- No .... *Helodrilus oculatus* (p. 36)

17. Does the clitellum start on:

- Segments 25, 26 or 27 .... Go to question 18
- Segments 28, 29 or 30 .... Go to question 20

18. Does the TP start before segment 30?

- Yes .... *Dendrodrilus rubidus* (p. 35)

- No .... Go to question 19

19. Is the worm is over 5 cm long?

- Yes .... *Dendrobaena veneta* (p. 35)

- No .... *Dendrobaena hortensis* (p. 33)

20. Does the TP end on segment 32?

- Yes .... *Dendrobaena attemsi* (p. 33)

- No .... Go to question 21

Check: *D. attemsi* is a small worm usually found in acid woodlands.

21. Does the clitellum span:

- Segments 29 or 34 .... *Octolasion cyaneum* (p. 41)

- Segments 30 to 35 .... *Octolasion lacteum* (p. 41)

Check: *O. cyaneum* a larger bluey grey worm with a clitellum starting on segment 29.

O. lacteum has a clitellum starting on segment 30, TP extends the whole length of the clitellum.

22. Does the TP start on:

- Segments 33 to 34 .... *Satchellius mammalis* (p. 42)

- TP absent or starting on segments 35, 36 or 37 ....
  .... Go to question 23

Check: these are both small worms. Maximum size 45 mm.

23. Are the setae:

- Closely paired .... *Apporectodea icterica* (p. 30)

- Widely paired .... *Dendrobaena pygmaea* (p. 34)

Check: *A. icterica* is a greyish worm with a clitellum on segments 33-34 to 42-44. *D. pygmaea* is a very small reddish worm with a clitellum on segments 32-33 to 37-38.

Table 2.

Quick earthworm comparison chart						
Earthworm	Head shape	Setae spacing	Colour (can be variable)	Clitellum	TP	TP shape
Allolobophora chlorotica	epi	closely	pink or green	28-29 to 37	31, 33, 35	sucker-like discs or 3 distinct mounds
Allolobophoridella eiseni	tany	closely	dull red	24-25 to 32-33	none	n/a
Aporrectodea caliginosa	epi	closely	usually pinky grey, occasionally large worm with very deep red head resembling *A. longa*	variable starting anywhere from 25 but usually 27 to 34-36	31-33	2 humps
Aporrectodea cupulifera	epi	closely	pinky grey	25-26 to 32	28, 30 (can also span part of 27 & 31)	2 sucker-like discs or 2 distinct mounds
Aporrectodea icterica	epi	closely	usually grey	33-34 to 42-43 (rarely 44)	35-36 to 42-43	long thin band sometimes hard to differentiate
Aporrectodea limicola	epi	closely	usually grey	28-29 to 35-36	33-34	2 humps
Aporrectodea longa	epi	closely	very dark head almost black	27-28 to 35-36	31 but usually 32-34	band
Aporrectodea rosea	epi	closely	grey/pink	25-26 to 32-33 can be flared	29-31 or only 29-30	raised band
Dendrobaena attemsi	epi	widely	rosy to red loses colour very quickly when preserved	28-29 to 34	30-32	raised band
Dendrobaena hortensis	epi	widely	red	26-27 to 33	30 to 31-half 32	swelling
Dendrobaena pygmaea	epi	widely	variable	32-33 to 37-38	usually absent	ridge (if present)

epi = epilobic head
tany = tanylobic head

Continued

Key to the earthworms of the UK and Ireland

Earthworm	Head shape	Setae spacing	Colour (can be variable)	Clitellum	TP	TP shape
Dendrobaena octaedra	epi	widely	red	27-29 to 33-34	31-33	usually a thin band otherwise a raised area
Dendrobaena veneta	epi	widely	red	26-27 to 32-33	29-30 to 31-32	swelling
Dendrodrilus rubidus	epi	widely	red	25-27 to 32-33	28-29 to 30	swelling
Eisenia fetida	epi	closely	red with striped appearance when stretched	24-26 to 32 (occasionally 33 or 34)	27-28 to 30-31	thin bands
Eiseniella tetraedra	epi	closely	pale	22-23 to 26-27	22-23 to 26-27	band
Helodrilus oculatus	epi	closely	pale	21-22 to 32	29 to 30	ridge
Lumbricus castaneus	tany	closely	red	27-28 to 33-34	29 to 32	band
Lumbricus festivus	tany	closely	red	33-34 to 40	35 to 38	band
Lumbricus friendi	tany	closely	red	32-33 to 38	34 to 36	thin ridge
Lumbricus rubellus	tany	closely	red	26-27 to 32	28 to 31	thick band
Lumbricus terrestris	tany	closely	red	32-37	32-33 to 36-37	ridge
Microscolex phosphoreus	epi	patterns different	can be phosphorescent usually light in colour	13 to 17	n/a	n/a
Murchieona muldali	epi	closely	pinky grey	26-27 to 33-34	unlikely to be present	absent
Octolasion cyneum	epi	widely after saddle	blue-grey	29 to 34	29-30 to 33-34	band
Octolasion lacteum	epi	widely after saddle	variable usually greyish	30 to 35	30-31 to 34-35	band
Satchellius mammalis	epi	widely	red	31 to 36	33 to 34	often a semi circular raised band
Sparganophilus tamesis	epi	closely	pink	14-14 to 26	15-19 to 22-24	variable

Species Accounts

27 species are included in the following pages. The photographs are taken from specimens housed at the Natural History Museum London. They are all preserved specimens so natural colour is not maintained. The colour of the worm in life is noted. A scale bar is included on all pictures. Each white line represents 1 mm.

The information included on the species pages was drawn together from the Soil Biodiversity group at Natural History Museum London (including a report for Natural England), the collections of the Natural History Museum, Sims and Gerard (1999) and Csuzdi and Zicsi's (2003) publication on the earthworms of Hungary.

An indication is given as to how rare or common the earthworm is. 'Patchy' means that it is generally rare but can be common in specific habitats. Note that still not enough is known about earthworm distributions around the UK and Ireland (Carpenter *et al*, 2011).

Allolobophora chlorotica (Savigny, 1826)

Very common

Ecological group: endogeic

Colour in life: two colour morphs exist: pink and green

Habitat: found in the majority of habitats but prefers neutral to base rich grasslands and arable soils. Not usually found in the most acidic woodlands such as pine. There are said to be some habitat differences between the colour morphs:

Pink form. Mainly found in woodlands and gardens. Prefers drier conditions than the green morph

Green form. Found in many habitats but dominant in grassland, prefers wetter conditions

External characters

Male pores: segment 15 encroaching onto 14 and 16

Clitellum: starts rarely on 28 usually 29 through to 37

TP: sucker like lumps on segments 31, 33 and 35

Setae: closely paired

Head: epilobic

Length: 30-80 mm; **diameter**: 2-7 mm

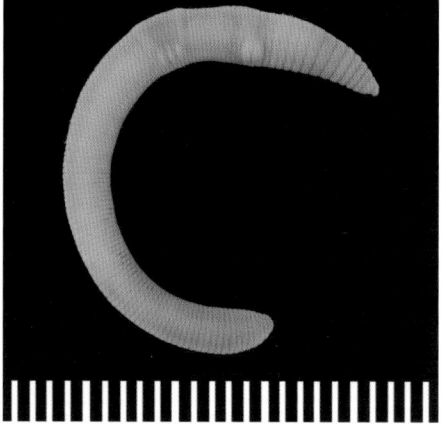

Allolobophoridella eiseni (Levinsen, 1884)

Rare

Ecological group: epigeic

Colour in life: dull reddish or brownish dorsally

Habitat: acidic soils mainly, prevalent in moorland, bogs and broadleaf woodlands, usually under bark

External characters

Male pores: segment 15

Clitellum: variable, starting anywhere from 25 but usually 27 to 34-36

TP: not present

Setae: closely paired

Head: tanylobic

Length: 30-64 mm; **diameter**: 2-5 mm

Aporrectodea caliginosa (Savigny, 1826)

Very common

Ecological group: endogeic

Colour in life: grey/pinky

Habitat: found in most habitats, very dominant in grasslands. Not found in the most acidic environments generally such as heathlands and mires. Seems a little more disturbance tolerant than *Allolobophora chlorotica*

External characters

Male pores: segment 15 often encroaching onto 14 and 16

Clitellum: this can start as early as 25 but usually is on segments 29 through to 34 or 35

TP: 2 humps on segments 31-33

Setae: closely paired

Head: epilobic

Length: 40-180 mm; **diameter**: 2-7 mm;

Aporrectodea cupulifera (Tetry, 1937)

Very rare

Ecological group: endogeic

Colour in life: grey/pink occasionally very deep red head resembling *A. longa*

Habitat: only recorded in Southern Ireland

External characters

Male pores: segment 15

Clitellum: starts on 25 or usually 26 through to 32

TP: lumps, can be 'sucker like' on segments 28 and 30, or span part of 27 through to 31

Setae: closely paired

Head: epilobic

Length: 35-50 mm

Aporrectodea icterica (Savigny, 1826)

Rare

Ecological group: endogeic

Colour in life: usually grey, but can be variable; yellows, grey or sometimes with a brown tint

Habitat: found in grasslands and orchards

External characters

Male pores: segment 15 often encroaching onto segments 14 and 16

Clitellum: 33 or 34 through to 42-43 (rarely 44)

TP: narrow bands 35 or 36 through to 42 or 43

Setae: closely paired

Head: epilobic

Length: 50-140 mm; **diameter**: 3-6 mm

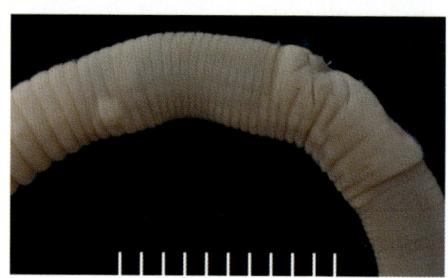

Aporrectodea limicola (Michaelsen, 1890)

Rare

Ecological group: endogeic
Colour in life: greyish colour with pinky anterior
Habitat: waterlogged soils

External characters

Male pores: segment 15, encroaching onto segments 14 and 16

Clitellum: starts rarely on segment 28 normally 29-35 sometimes extends to 36

TP: 2 humps like that of *A. caliginosa* **but** on segments 33 and 34

Setae: closely paired
Head: epilobic
Length: 40-100 mm; **diameter**: 3-4 mm

Aporrectodea longa (Ude, 1885)

Common

Ecological group: anecic
Colour in life: distinctive black head
Habitat: most abundant in grassland and gardens

External characters

Male pores: segment 15 occasionally encroaching onto 14 and 16

Clitellum: starts on 27 or 28 and extends through to 35 or 36

TP: occasionally starting 31 but usually 32 through to 34

Setae: closely paired
Head: epilobic
Length: 90-170 mm; **diameter**: 4-9 mm

Aporrectodea rosea (Savigny, 1826)

Common

Ecological group: endogeic

Colour in life: grey/pink

Habitat: universal, often found in woodland and grassland. Prefers neutral and base rich soils.

External characters

Male pores: segment 15 occasionally encroaching onto 16

Clitellum: can start as early as segment 23 but usually found on 25 or 26 through to 32 or 33

TP: usually a raised bump on segments 29 to 30-31, occasionally only showing on half of segment 31

Setae: closely paired

Head: epilobic

Length: 20-110 mm; **diameter**: 2-6 mm

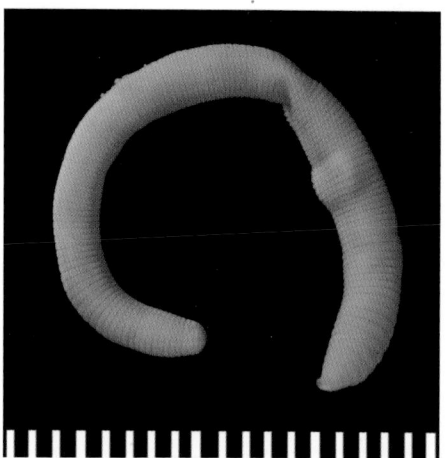

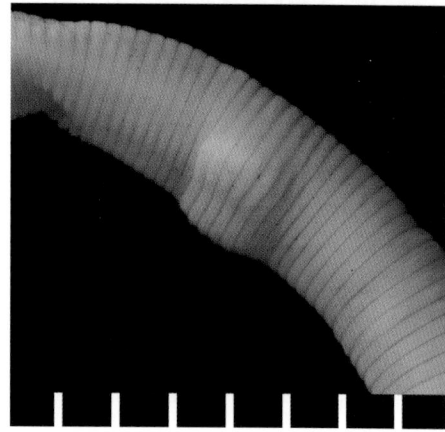

Dendrobaena attemsi (Michaelsen, 1902)

Rare

Ecological group: epigeic

Colour in life: darkish red dorsally or pale. Once preserved loses colour very quickly

Habitat: acidic woodlands in Southern England.

External characters

Male pores: segment 15 very occasionally encroaching onto 16

Clitellum: 28 or usually 29 to 34

TP: raised band on 30-32

Setae: widely paired

Head: epilobic

Length: 26-70 mm; **diameter**: 1-3 mm

Dendrobaena hortensis (Michaelsen, 1890)

Rare

Ecological group: epigeic

Colour in life: variable colour; reddish generally at front end turning paler to white

Habitat: mainly found in broadleaf woodland on acidic soils and frequent in compost, much more abundant in Southern Europe

External characters

Male pores: segment 15

Clitellum: occasionally starts on 26 usually 27-33

TP: a raised band on 30 and 31, occasionally starting on 29 and extending onto 32

Setae: widely paired

Head: epilobic

Length: 20-50 mm; **diameter**: 1.5-5 mm

Dendrobaena octaedra (Savigny, 1826)

Rare (but can be abundant in certain areas)

Ecological group: epigeic

Colour in life: dark red before clitellum dorsally, pale ventrally

Habitat: prefers broadleaf woodland on acidic soils

External characters

Male pores: segment 15

Clitellum: 27 or 28 but usually 29 through to 33 or 34

TP: usually a distinctive thin band, but sometimes a raised area in 31-33

Setae: widely paired

Head: epilobic

Length: 20-60 mm; **diameter**: 2-5 mm

Dendrobaena pygmaea (Savigny, 1826)

Very rare

Ecological group: epigeic

Colour in life: variable, some lightly coloured with a reddish or greyish tint, others unpigmented

Habitat: well drained soils and some broadleaf woodlands

External characters

Male pores: segment 15

Clitellum: 32 or 33 through to 36

TP: usually not present. If present ridge in 35-37

Setae: widely paired

Head: epilobic

Length: 15-45 mm; **diameter**: 0.5-1.2 mm

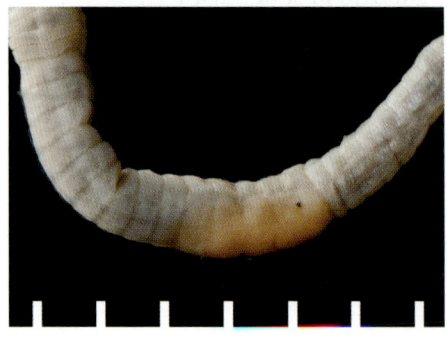

Dendrobaena veneta (Rosa, 1886)

Rare (common in worm farms in UK)

Ecological group: compost worm/epigeic
Colour in life: dark red dorsally
Habitat: compost heaps and sewage beds

External characters

Male pores: segment 15

Clitellum: occasionally starting on 26 usually 27 to 32-33

TP: rarely starting on 29 usually 30-31 where can look a little circular (see photograph right). Can extend onto half 32

Setae: widely paired

Head: epilobic

Length: 50-155 mm; **diameter**: 4-8 mm

Dendrodrilus rubidus (Savigny, 1826)

Common

Ecological group: epigeic
Colour in life: deep red on dorsal surface
Habitat: often found in woodland in microhabitats. Likes high organic content and acidic soils. Can be found in wood ant nests

External characters

Male pores: segment 15, encroaching onto segments 14 and 16 in some cases

Clitellum: very rarely starts on 25 usually 26 or 27 through to 31-32

TP: on 29 and 30 sometimes looks like 4 squares; 2 on each side. Sometimes on 28 as well

Setae: widely paired

Head: epilobic

Length: 20-100 mm; **diameter**: 2-6 mm

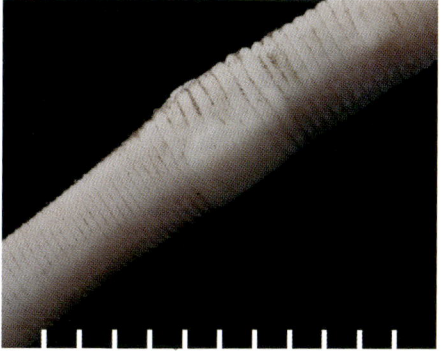

Eisenia fetida (Savigny, 1826)

Common (in compost)

Ecological group: compost worm/epigeic

Colour in life: dark in colour dorsally from head to tail – when moving gives a striped appearance

Habitat: compost bins, places with very high organic matter

External characters

Male pores: segment 15

Clitellum: starting on 24, 25, 26 or usually 27 and extending through to 32, sometimes onto 33 or even 34

TP: thin bands running from 27 or mainly 28 through to 30 or 31, occasionally onto 32

Setae: closely paired

Head: epilobic

Length: 26-130 mm; **diameter**: 2-6 mm

Eiseniella tetraedra (Savigny, 1826)

Common

Ecological group: endogeic
Colour in life: pale worm
Habitat: waterlogged soils

External characters

Male pores: usually on 13 (very rarely on 11, 12, 14 or 15)

Tail: a 'square' shape

Clitellum: 22-23 to 26-27

TP: long thin bands on 23-26 occasionally extending onto 22 and 27

Setae: closely paired

Head: epilobic

Length: 20-80 mm; **diameter**: 1.5-4 mm

Helodrilus oculatus Hoffmeister, 1845

Very rare

Ecological group: endogeic

Colour in life: pale worm occasionally with some black markings

Habitat: waterlogged soils especially broadleaf woodlands. Prefers alkaline conditions

External characters

Male pores: segment 15 extending onto segments 14 and 16 (very large)

Clitellum: occasionally starting on 21 usually 22 through to 32

TP: ridge on 29 and 30

Setae: closely paired

Head: epilobic

Length: 35-80 mm; **diameter**: 1-2 mm

Lumbricus castaneus (Savigny, 1826)

Common

Ecological group: anecic

Colour in life: deep red anteriorly

Habitat: prefers dryer basic soils, although can be found in most habitats. Often found in grassland, woodland and hedgerows

External characters

Male pores: segment 15 (very small)

Clitellum: 28-33 but sometimes encroaches onto 27 and 34

TP: bands on 29-32

Setae: closely paired

Head: tanylobic

Length: 30-85 mm; **diameter**: 2-5 mm

Lumbricus festivus (Savigny, 1826)

Rare

Ecological group: epigeic
Colour in life: deep red anteriorly
Habitat: prefers grasslands and arable fields

External characters

Male pores: segment 15
Clitellum: starting on 33 or 34 through to segment 40
TP: bands 35-38
Setae: closely paired
Head: tanylobic
Length: 48-110mm; **diameter**: 3.5-6 mm

Lumbricus friendi Cognetti, 1904

Very rare

Ecological group: anecic
Colour in life: purplish red dorsally
Habitat: woodlands, grasslands and very moist conditions. Very few British records

External characters

Male pores: segment 15 occasionally encroaching slightly onto segments 14 and 16
Clitellum: half 32-33 through to 37-38
TP: thin ridge 34-36
Setae: closely paired
Head: tanylobic
Length: 90-200 mm; **diameter**: 4-8 mm

Lumbricus rubellus Hoffmeister, 1845

Common

Ecological group: epigeic

Colour in life: purplish red dorsally

Habitat: Recorded from all habitats, particularly prevalent in organic-rich environments such as under dung as well as in acid grassland and woodland. However, seems to have the lowest habitat specificity of all British earthworms

External characters

Male pores: segment 15 (small)

Clitellum: 26 or 27 through to 32

TP: occasional part of segment 27 but mainly 28-32

Setae: closely paired

Head: tanylobic

Length: 25-150 mm; **diameter**: 3-6 mm

Lumbricus terrestris Linnaeus, 1758

Common

Ecological group: anecic

Colour in life: deep purplish red dorsally

Habitat: mainly found in grasslands and lawns, especially when undisturbed. Preference for alkaline conditions, especially clay

External characters

Male pores: segment 15 often encroaching onto segments 14 and 16

Clitellum: 31 or 32 through to 37

TP: 32 or 33 through to 36 or 37. A thick band, can be 'canoe' shaped

Setae: closely paired

Head: tanylobic

Length: 90-350 mm; **diameter**: 6-10 mm

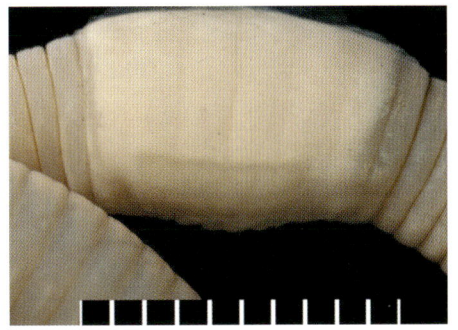

Microscolex phosphoreus (Dugès, 1837)

Rare

Ecological group: endogeic

Colour in life: can give off an bioluminescence at night

Habitat: found in areas of high organic matter such as compost heaps and also found on golf courses

External characters

Male pores: segment 17

Clitellum: 13-17 and a very different shape to that of the Lumbricidae family of which most of the British fauna is part

TP: not present but male and prosthetic pores on 17 and female pores often visible on 14

Setae: patterns different

Head: epilobic

Length: 10-35 mm; **diameter**: 1-1.5 mm

Murchieona muldali (Omodeo, 1956)

Rare

Ecological group: endogeic

Colour in life: pinky grey

Habitat: preference for areas with a high moisture content and pH, can be found in woodland and grassland; particularly abundant in field margins

External characters

Male pores: segment 15 encroaching onto segments 14 and 16

Clitellum: 26-27 to 33-34

TP: unlikely to be present

Setae: closely paired

Head: epilobic

Length: 10-60 mm; **diameter**: 1.2-2 mm

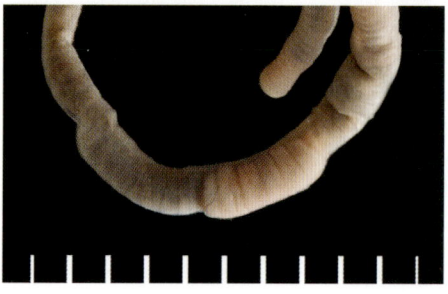

Octolasion cyaneum (Savigny, 1826)

Common

Ecological group: endogeic

Colour in life: no pigmentation or a light blue-grey

Habitat: prefers wet conditions, can be found in most habitats

External characters

Male pores: segment 15

Clitellum: 29-34

TP: white bands on 30-33, although occasionally can start on 29 and extend to 34

Setae: very small and difficult to see often more closely paired at the anterior but widely paired in the posterior region

Head: epilobic

Length: 65-140 mm; **diameter**: 5-8 mm

Octalasion lacteum (Örley, 1881)

Common

Ecological group: endogeic

Colour in life: variable usually greyish

Habitat: preference for very moist habitats

External characters

Male pores: segment 15 encroaching onto segments 14 and 16

Clitellum: 30-35

TP: half 30, 31-34, half 35

Setae: more closely paired anteriorally but widely paired posteriorly

Head: epilobic

Length: 25-160 mm; **diameter**: 2.5-6 mm

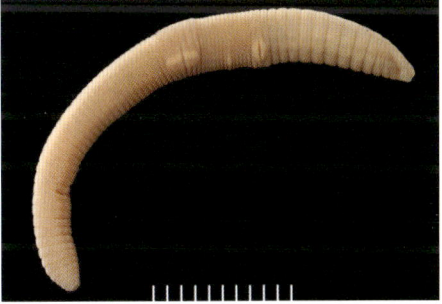
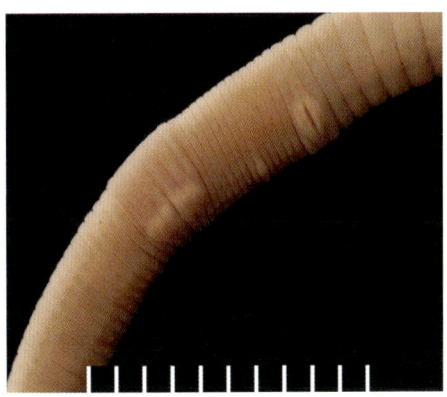

Satchellius mammalis (Savigny, 1826)

Common

Ecological group: epigeic

Colour in life: deep red in life

Habitat: found in woodlands, areas of high organic matter and on river banks. Prefers basic conditions

External characters

Male pores: segment 15 encroaching onto segments 14 and 16

Clitellum: 31-36

TP: often a semi circular raised band on 33 and 34

Setae: widely paired

Head: epilobic

Length: 24-41 mm; **diameter**: 1.5-3 mm

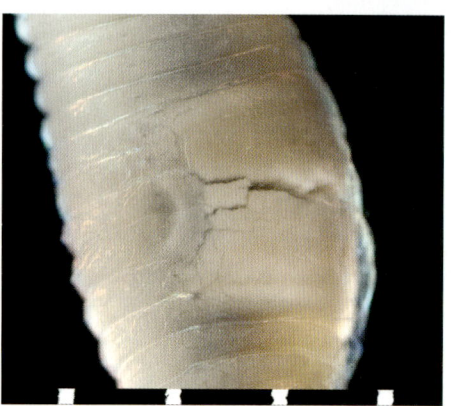

Sparganophilus tamesis Benham, 1892

Possibly not present

Ecological group: endogeic; although does not appear to conform as well to the groupings. The author of the species believes they stay deep in wet mud for much of the year coming to the surface among the roots of plants during the summer months for reproduction

Colour in life: pale pinkish

Habitat: found in saturated soils and river beds. The most aquatic of the earthworms

External characters

Male pores: segment 19 (inconspicuous)

Clitellum: 14 or 15 through to 26

TP: present along most of the clitellum but can be variable, always present on 19-22, usually 15-24

Setae: closely paired

Head: epilobic

Length: 70-200 mm; **diameter**: 1-5 mm

REFERENCES AND FURTHER READING

BEDDARD, F.E. (1890). Exhibition of and remarks upon, some living specimens of oriental earthworms, found in a greenhouse in Scotland. *Proceedings of the Zoological Society London* **1890**, 94.

BEDDARD, F.E. (1891). On the structure of two new genera of earthworms belonging to the Eudrilidae and remarks on Nematodrilus. *Quarterly Journal of Microscipical Science* **32**, 235-278.

BEDDARD, F.E. (1892). On some species of the genus Perichaeta (sensu stricta). *Proceedings of the Zoological Society of London* **1892**, 153-172

BEDDARD, F.E. (1893). On some new species of earthworms from various parts of the world. *Proceedings of the Zoological Society of London* **1892**, 666-706.

BEDDARD, F.E. (1901). Contributions to the knowledge and systematic arrangement of earthworms. *Proceedings of the Zoological Society of London* **1901**, 187-286.

BEDDARD, F.E. (1906) Annelida, Oligochaeta. *Kew Bulletin Additional Series* **5**, 66-68.

BLAKEMORE, R.J. (2005). *British and Irish Earthworms: a checklist of species*. [online] Available at www.annelida.net/earthworms/Britain & Ireland.pdf [accessed 13 February 2012].

BLAKEMORE, R.J. (2008). Seeking consensus on main categories of ecological strategies of earthworms. *Advances in Earthworm Taxonomy III. Proceedings of the 3rd International Oligochaete taxonomy meeting*. Nicosia, Cyprus 2-6 April 2007, pp 131-136.

BOUCHÉ, M.B. (1971). Relation entre les structures spatiales et fonctionnelles des écosystèmes illustrés par le rôle pédobiologique des vers de terre. In PESSON, P. (ed.) *La vie des sols*. Paris: Gauthier-Villars, pp 187-209.

BOUCHÉ, M.B. (1972). *Lombriciens de France. Ecologie et systematique*. Paris: INRA.

BOUCHÉ, M.B. (1977) - Stratégies lombriciennes. In : LOHM, U. and PERSSON, T. (eds) *Soil organisms as components of ecosystems*. Stockholm: Ecology Bulletin/NFR, **25**, 122-132.

BUTT, K. R. and GRIGOROPOULOU, N. (2010). Basic Research Tools for Earthworm Ecology. *Applied and Environmental Soil Science*, vol. 2010, Article ID 562816, 12 pages, 2010. doi:10.1155/2010/562816.

CARPENTER, D., SHERLOCK, E., JONES D.T., CHIMINOIDES, J., WRITER, T., NIELSON, A., BOAG, B., KEITH, A.M. and EGGLETON, P. (2011). Mapping of earthworm distribution for the British Isles and Eire highlights the underrecording of an ecologically important group. *Biodiversity and Conservation* **21**, 475-485.

ČERNOSVITOV, L. and EVANS, A.C. (1947). Lumbricidae (Annelida). With a key to the common species. *Synopses of the British Fauna* **6**. London: Linnean Society of London.

CSUZDI, C. and PAVLICEK, T. (2002). *Murchieona miniscula*, a newly recorded earthworm from Israel and distribution of the genera Dendrobaena and Bimastos in Israel. *Zoology in the Middle East* **25**, 105-114.

CSUZDI, C. and ZICSI, A. (2003). *Earthworms of Hungary (Annelida: Oligochaeta; Lumbricidae)*. Budapest: Hungarian Natural History Museum.

CSUZDI, C., SZLAVECZ, K. (2003). *Lumbricus friendi* Cognetti 1904, a new exotic earthworm in North America. *Northeastern Naturalist* **10** (1) 77-82.

EDWARDS, C.A. ed. (2004). *Earthworm Ecology*. (2nd ed.). Boca Raton: CRC Press LLC.

EDWARDS, C.A. and BOHLEN, P.J. (1996). *Biology and ecology of earthworms*. (3rd ed.). London: Chapman and Hall.

FRIEND, H. (1891). Earthworms of the North of England. *The Naturalist, Hull* **16**, 13-15.

FRIEND, H. (1911). New British enchytraeids. *Journal of the Royal Microscopical Society*. **31**, 730-736.

FRIEND, H. (1916). Alien Oligochaets in England. *Journal of the Royal Microscopical Society*. **36**, 262–271.

FRIEND, H. (1923). *British earthworms and how to identify them*. London: Epworth Press.

FRIEND, H. (1924). *The story of British annelids*. London: Epworth Press.

GERARD, B.M. (1964). British Lumbricidae. *Synopses of the British Fauna* **6**. London: Linnean Society of London.

GUNN, A. (1992). The use of mustard to estimate earthworm populations. *Pedobiologia* **36**, 65-67.

LEE, K.E. (1959). The earthworm fauna of New Zealand. *New Zealand Department of Scientific and Industrial Research Bulletin* **130**.

LEE, K.E. (1985). *Earthworms: their ecology and relationships with soils and land use*. Sydney: Academic Press Sydney.

LOWE, C.N. and BUTT, K.R. (2008). Preliminary evidence for the adoption of *Allolobophora virescens* (Savigny, 1826). *Advances in Earthworm Taxonomy III. Proceedings of the 3rd International Oligochaete taxonomy meeting*. Nicosia, Cyprus 2-6 April 2007, pp 63-39.

MULDOWNEY, J. and SCHMIDT, O. (2002). *Allolobophora cupulifera* in Ireland: First records for the British Isles. *Megadrilogica* **9** (5) 29-32

SATCHELL, J.E. (1967). Colour dimorphism in *Allolobophora chlorotica* Sav. (Lumbricidae). *Journal of Animal Ecology* **36**: 623-630.

SHERLOCK, E. and CARPENTER, D. (2009). An updated earthworm list for the British Isles and two new 'exotic' species to Britain from Kew Gardens. *European Journal of Soil Biology* **45**, 431-435.

SHERLOCK, E. and JONES, D. (2008). A field guide to British earthworms to support a national survey. *Advances in Earthworm Taxonomy III. Proceedings of the 3rd International Oligochaete taxonomy meeting*. Nicosia, Cyprus 2-6 April 2007, pp 225-228.

SIMS, R.W. and GERARD, B.M. (1985). Earthworms. *Synopses of the British Fauna (New Series)* **39**. London: Linnean Society of London.

SIMS, R.W. and GERARD, B.M. (1999). Earthworms. *Synopses of the British Fauna (New Series)* **39**. London: Linnean Society of London.